121

ALTERNATOR BOOKS™

SURVIVING
A SHARK ATTACK

BETHANY HAMILTON

KATIE MARSICO

Lerner Publications ◆ Minneapolis

To my Maria, as well as the Cummins girls
(all truly brave in their own right)

Lerner Publications Company
A division of Lerner Publishing Group, Inc.
241 First Avenue North
Minneapolis, MN 55401 USA

For reading levels and more information, look up this title at www.lernerbooks.com.

Library of Congress Cataloging-in-Publication Data

Names: Marsico, Katie, 1980– author.
Title: Surviving a shark attack : Bethany Hamilton / by Katie Marsico.
Description: Minneapolis, Minnesota : Lerner Publications Company, [2018] | Series:
    They survived (Alternator Books) | Includes bibliographical references and
    index. | Audience: Ages: 8–12. | Audience: Grades: 4 to 6.
Identifiers: LCCN 2018008679 (print) | LCCN 2018028103 (ebook) |
    ISBN 9781541525610 (eb pdf) | ISBN 9781541523531 (library binding : alk. paper)
Subjects: LCSH: Hamilton, Bethany—Juvenile literature. | Women surfers—
    Hawaii—Kauai—Biography—Juvenile literature. | Surfers—Hawaii—Kauai—
    Biography—Juvenile literature. | Amputees—Hawaii—Kauai—Biography—
    Juvenile literature. | Shark attacks—Juvenile literature.
Classification: LCC GV838.H36 (ebook) | LCC GV838.H36 M37 2018 (print) |
    DDC 797.3/2092 [B]—dc23

LC record available at https://lccn.loc.gov/2018008679

Manufactured in the United States of America
1-44426-34685-7/5/2018

CONTENTS

SURROUNDED BY A SEA OF RED

When Bethany Hamilton looked at the water around her, she saw it had turned blood red. Moments before, the ocean had been calm and clear off the northern coast of the Hawaiian island of Kauai. The thirteen-year-old surfer had been hoping to catch some waves with friends on October 31, 2003. Yet her plans suddenly took a life-changing turn.

Bethany, who was lying on her surfboard, didn't see the tiger shark rush toward her. She felt pressure and a powerful tugging as its teeth ripped into her left arm. In just seconds the shark let go and disappeared beneath the waves. Before it did, however, it tore off most of Bethany's left arm. When Bethany's friends realized what had happened, they began pulling her toward shore roughly a quarter mile (0.4 km) away. But they couldn't just drag her board across the foamy waves. Her rescuers also had to prevent her from bleeding to death.

The trip to shore was filled with risk, uncertainty, and several unspoken questions. Was the shark still nearby? What was the fastest way to get help? Most important, would Bethany survive?

CHAPTER 1

NO WARNING SIGNS IN SIGHT

Even as a child, Bethany felt at home in the cool, turquoise waters surrounding Kauai. Like her family, she enjoyed surfing. By the age of eight, she had begun winning surfing competitions.

Actress AnnaSophia Robb as Bethany
in the 2011 movie *Soul Surfer*

Bethany's abilities even earned her **sponsors**. But she viewed surfing as far more than winning trophies and earning money. She also saw it as a fun and exciting opportunity to conquer new challenges. "I'd say [Bethany] has salt in her blood," longtime family friend and fellow surfer Suzanne "Bobo" Bollins said. "She lives and breathes the ocean. She gets the big waves."

Bethany looked forward to riding the biggest, most challenging waves. It's why she and her friends, the

Blanchards, headed to Tunnels Beach as the sun rose on Halloween day in 2003. They wanted to tackle the monster 80-foot (24 m) waves that rose along Kauai's northern coast.

Like Bethany, the Blanchards were experienced surfers. Alana Blanchard was also thirteen. She and Bethany were best friends and often surfed together. That morning Alana's father, Holt, and her fifteen-year-old brother, Byron, joined them.

Alana Blanchard became a professional surfer. She surfs in competitions around the world.

AnnaSophia Robb depicts the calm moments surfing just before the attack in a scene from *Soul Surfer*.

It was too early for lifeguards to be on duty at Tunnels Beach when Bethany and the Blanchards arrived. Yet they had early-morning surf sessions often, and they knew the best way to stay safe was to go out as a group.

Bethany and her friends paddled away from the shoreline and passed a **reef** to get out to the open ocean. Then they waited for the surf to pick up. While Bethany searched for signs that larger waves might be rolling in, she stretched out sideways on her board. She looked around but saw no hints of the danger **lurking** nearby.

CHAPTER 2
WOUNDED IN OPEN WATER

Bethany was relaxed. She dangled her left arm over the edge of her board. Before she knew what was happening a 14- to 15-foot (4.3 to 4.6 m) tiger shark swam up to her. Almost immediately, she felt a crushing pressure on her left arm.

Instinctively, Bethany grabbed her board with her right hand to avoid being pulled underwater. Instead of dragging her down, the shark tugged her back and forth. Bethany didn't scream or splash, and the shark disappeared within seconds. But the attack had been long enough to cause serious damage.

Sharks don't often attack humans. When they do, it is usually because the shark confuses the human with their natural prey such as seals or sea lions.

A fireman shows off the huge shark bite in Bethany's surfboard.

When Bethany looked down, she noticed that a large crescent-shaped chunk of her board was missing. Yet a far more terrible sight awaited her. The shark had torn Bethany's left arm from her body about 4 inches (10 cm) beneath her shoulder. Blood gushed freely from the wound and clouded the waves around her.

Amazingly, Bethany didn't feel pain. The sudden violence of the attack likely had left her in **shock**, which can sometimes prevent a person from feeling pain. Bethany managed to stay calm and paddled toward the Blanchards.

BETHANY ON THE BIG SCREEN

In 2004 Bethany published her autobiography *Soul Surfer*. The movie *Soul Surfer* followed in 2011. AnnaSophia Robb played Bethany, but the real Bethany made several on-screen appearances. She even played herself for some of the surfing scenes. The cast and crew also headed to the actual location of the shark attack to re-create that key moment.

AnnaSophia Robb and Bethany became close friends during the filming of *Soul Surfer*.

Holt Blanchard helped save Bethany's life after the shark attack. In the movie *Soul Surfer*, Blanchard was played by Kevin Sorbo (*right*).

When Bethany called out that she had been bitten, Holt Blanchard thought she was joking. He hadn't noticed her struggling or panicking. "[Then] I saw blood in the water, and I realized she did get attacked," he said later. "I paddled up to her, and at that point I noticed her arm was gone." Holt's disbelief turned to horror when he realized how much blood Bethany was losing. He feared that she'd die if she didn't receive medical treatment. Before the Blanchards could get Bethany to a hospital, however, they needed to help her out of the water.

CHAPTER 3
BACK TO THE BEACH

Though Bethany had suffered serious blood loss, she didn't lose **consciousness**. Since she was alert, she could cling to her board. But the situation was still very serious.

Bethany and the Blanchards had to make it past the reef to get back to the shore at Tunnels Beach.

Holt realized he had to do something to slow her bleeding. They were still far from shore. The odds of Bethany surviving much more blood loss were not good. With no emergency supplies, he used his shirt to create a **tourniquet**. He wound it as tightly as he could around what remained of Bethany's left arm.

Byron swam ahead of everyone else. He planned to get a cell phone out of his family's truck and call 911. Meanwhile, Holt told Bethany to grab onto his swimsuit trunks. He then pulled her toward the shore. Alana paddled next to her father and Bethany. As Holt moved Bethany over the waves, he urged her to keep talking.

SURVIVAL GEAR

Tourniquets can be used in extreme survival situations to prevent serious blood loss. The tourniquet is put on the limb above the injury to stop the flow of blood to the wound. This helps slow the bleeding. Holt used his shirt to slow Bethany's blood loss, but most tourniquets are made from a stretchy piece of rubber or fabric.

"It was during this, the longest part of getting to the beach . . . that the fear began to wash over me," Bethany later said. "But I pushed any negative vibes away quickly with a prayer." Bethany forced herself to focus. Yet her blood loss and the shock of what she had just experienced made it difficult.

PACIFIC OCEAN

Bethany's surf spot

reef

reef

reef

reef

reef

Tunnels Beach

KAUAI NORTH SHORE

Finally, about twenty minutes after the attack, she was back on the sand. Thanks to Byron, an ambulance was on the way, but **paramedics** wouldn't arrive for a while. It was hard for an ambulance to get to Tunnels Beach fast.

Bethany started to fade in and out of consciousness. The tourniquet wasn't staying tied, so Holt replaced the shirt with a surfboard leash. That seemed to work better. Still, Bethany and her friends anxiously listened for sirens. Finally, paramedics arrived and took her to Wilcox Memorial Hospital in eastern Kauai. Soon after arriving, Bethany was taken into the operating room.

Curved roads around Tunnels Beach meant that Bethany's ambulance had to drive slowly.

AHEAD OF BETHANY AT THE HOSPITAL

Long before Byron dialed 911 from Tunnels, Bethany's father, Tom Hamilton, was waiting at Wilcox Memorial Hospital. But he didn't expect to see his daughter there. On the day of the attack, Tom checked into Wilcox for knee surgery. He was already in an operating room when someone burst in and put his surgery on hold. It was a moment he would never forget.

Paramedics had alerted the hospital that a thirteen-year-old female surfer was headed to the emergency room after being attacked by a shark. Tom knew right away that it was either Bethany or Alana. When the doctor confirmed it was Bethany, Tom was devastated.

Hospital staff said that they had to clear the operating room. They needed it for Bethany instead of her father. Nurses pushed his bed out and rushed Bethany into the room. She wasn't alert at the time. For Tom, it was an unbearable moment. As soon as she was out of surgery, he was among the first people by her side.

CHAPTER 4

LIFE AFTER THE ATTACK

Doctors at Wilcox Memorial Hospital fought to save Bethany's life. When she arrived there, she had lost more than 60 percent of her blood. Bethany required emergency surgery and blood **transfusions**. These procedures succeeded. Thanks to the Blanchards' quick thinking—and Bethany's ability to stay calm—she survived.

Only three weeks after the shark attack, Bethany was back on a surfboard! She knew that she would have to work harder to surf with one arm. Yet Bethany refused to allow her injury to keep her out of the water.

Bethany returned to the water in November 2003.

"Every time I would go out there, I would learn something new," Bethany recalled. "I kept practicing just on smaller waves . . . and each time I felt better and better about my surfing." She also relied heavily on the support of her family, friends, and a growing number of fans around the world. Bethany found comfort in her faith as well.

Bethany's father was a surfer too. He helped Bethany move forward after the attack.

In 2005 Bethany won her first national surfing title. She has since gained sponsors, claimed countless awards, and earned fame as a professional surfer. Bethany also runs her own foundation, Friends of Bethany. This organization offers help to a variety of people in need, including **amputees**.

Bethany uses her fame to help others. She especially likes to work with children.

Bethany married Adam Dirks ten years after her shark attack.

She got married in 2013, and she and her husband are raising their family in Kauai. Bethany and the Blanchards are still close friends.

Bethany continues to surf professionally. Her best performance came in the 2016 World Surfing League competition where she placed third, beating out world champions and top-ranked competitors.

To some, Bethany's story might seem like a tale shaped by the terror of a near-death experience. To her, however, it means far more. Bethany has turned her survival into a chance to celebrate life. She is proof that people can overcome incredible challenges.

SURVIVING DEADLY SITUATIONS

The ocean is an exciting place, but it can also test people's survival skills. Not all emergencies are the same. Yet if you ever face an emergency at sea, try the following tips:

1. Don't panic. Breathe deeply, count aloud, or talk to anyone who happens to be with you. Staying calm will make it easier to find a safe solution to your problem.

2. Use your energy wisely. Swimming against the tide will only make you tired and add to your challenges.

3. Be aware of your surroundings. Pay attention to the weather and anything you see around you that will help you track your location.

4. If you are already in a group, stay that way. There's greater safety in numbers. If you decide to split up, discuss when, where, and how you'll reconnect.

5. If you're alone, try to reach other people. Look for boaters, swimmers, surfers, or anyone on the beach.

6. Bethany Hamilton's story shows that people can overcome incredible odds. Should you need to prove your own survival skills, don't give up!

SOURCE NOTES

7 "Young Surfer Tells Tale of Shark Attack," *ABC News*, November 21, 2005, http://abcnews.go.com/2020/story?id =124360.

15 "Young Surfer."

19 Bethany Hamilton, *Soul Surfer* (New York: Simon & Schuster, 2004), 74.

24 "Surfer Girl Makes Comeback after Shark Attack," *ABC News*, April 7, 2005, http://abcnews.go.com/Primetime/Health /story?id=644247.

GLOSSARY

amputees: people who have lost a body part, usually as part of a surgery or for a specific medical reason

consciousness: the state of being awake and aware of one's surroundings

instinctively: reacting naturally without thinking or planning

lurking: threatening someone from a hidden or secret location

paramedics: people trained to provide emergency medical care, often during transport to a hospital

reef: a chain of rocks, coral, or sand near the surface of the water

shock: a serious medical condition that usually involves a sudden drop in blood pressure, which often occurs after severe blood loss or emotional stress

sponsors: organizations or businesses that pay for a sporting event in exchange for advertising rights

tourniquet: a tightly wound cord or bandage used for preventing blood loss

transfusions: medical treatments in which someone receives more blood

FURTHER INFORMATION

Bethany: Soul Surfer
http://bethanyhamilton.com

California Surf Museum—Courageous Inspiration: Bethany Hamilton
https://surfmuseum.org/exhibits/courageous-inspiration -bethany-hamilton/

Discovery Mindblown—Shark Attacks!
http://discoverymindblown.com/articles/shark-attacks/

Dubowski, Cathy East. *Shark Attack!* New York: DK, 2015.

Kidzworld—Bethany Hamilton Interview
http://www.kidzworld.com/article/5880-bethany-hamilton -interview

Mason, Paul. *The Shark Attack Files.* Minneapolis: Hungry Tomato, 2018.

Oxlade, Chris. *Be a Survivor.* Minneapolis: Lerner Publications, 2016.

Van Zee, Amy. *Bethany Hamilton: Shark Attack Survivor.* Mankato, MN: Child's World, 2016.

INDEX

PHOTO ACKNOWLEDGMENTS

Image credits: Felix Nendzig/Shutterstock.com, p. 1; Monica & Michael Sweet/ Getty Images, pp. 4–5; Jeffrey Mayer/WireImage/Getty Images, p. 5; Kicka Witte/ Design Pics/Getty Images, p. 6; AF archive/Sean McNamara Film Company/TriStar Pictures/Alamy Stock Photo, pp. 7, 9; Christophe Simon/AFP/Getty Images, p. 8; AleksandarNakic/Getty Images, p. 10; Jeff Rotman/Photolibrary/Getty Images, p. 11; AP Photo/Dennis Fujimoto, p. 12; Noel Vasquez/Getty Images, p. 13; Michael Patrick ONeill/Science Source/Getty Images, p. 14; RGR Collection/Alamy Stock Photo, p. 15; mihtiander/Getty Images, p. 16; Greg Vaughn/Getty Images, p. 17; Denisfilm/Getty Images, p. 18; Laura Westlund/Independent Picture Service, p. 19; Manuel Sulzer/Getty Images, p. 20; ChaNaWiT/Shutterstock.com, p. 22; Sport the Library/SportsChrome/Newscom, p. 23; Giulio Marcocchi/Getty Images, p. 24; Kirk Aeder/Icon SMI/Icon Sport Media/Getty Images, p. 25; Brian Ach/Stringery/Getty Images, p. 26; Mike McGregor/Stringer/Getty Images, p. 27; Tom Servais/AFP/ Getty Images, p. 28. Design elements: Miloje/Shutterstock.com; Redshinestudio/ Shutterstock.com; sl_photo/Shutterstock.com; Khvost/Shutterstock; Milan M/ Shutterstock.com.

Cover: Splash News/Alamy Stock Photo (Hamilton); Martin Prochazkacz/ Shutterstock.com (wave).